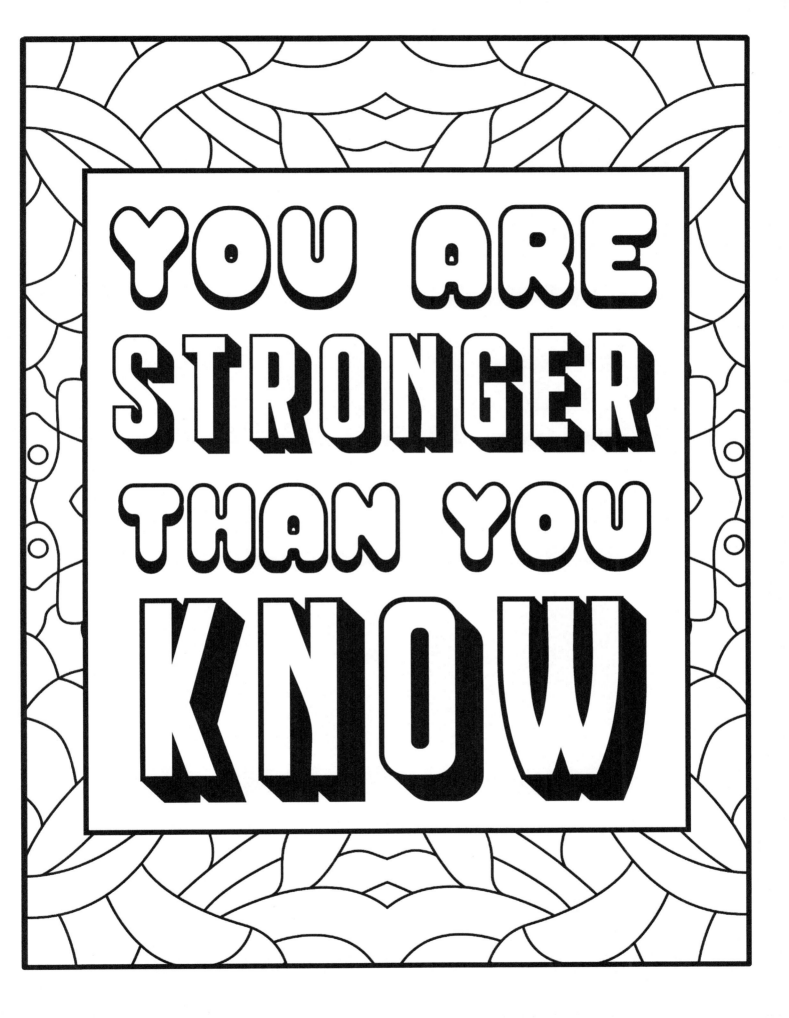

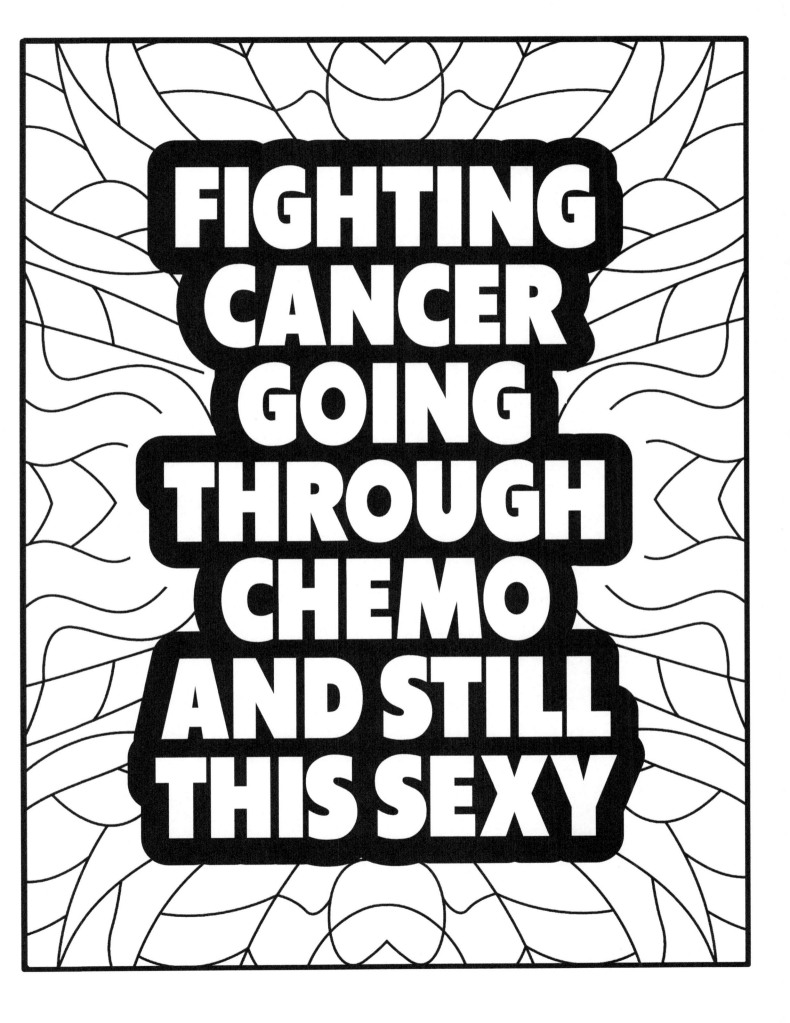

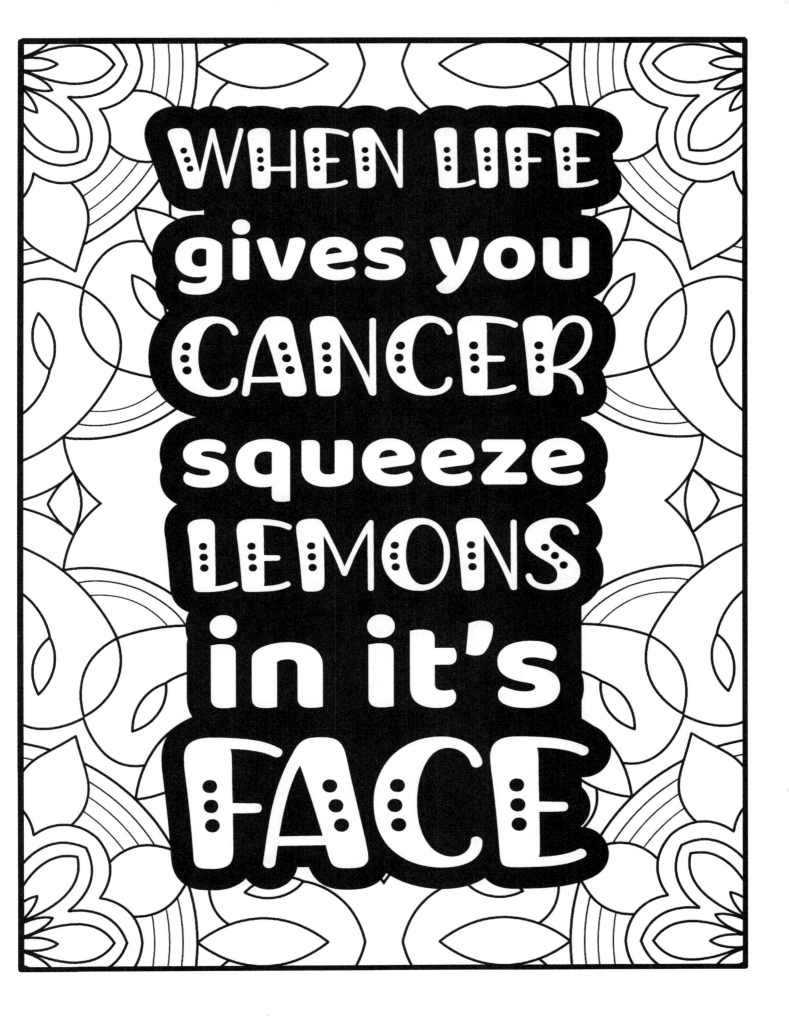

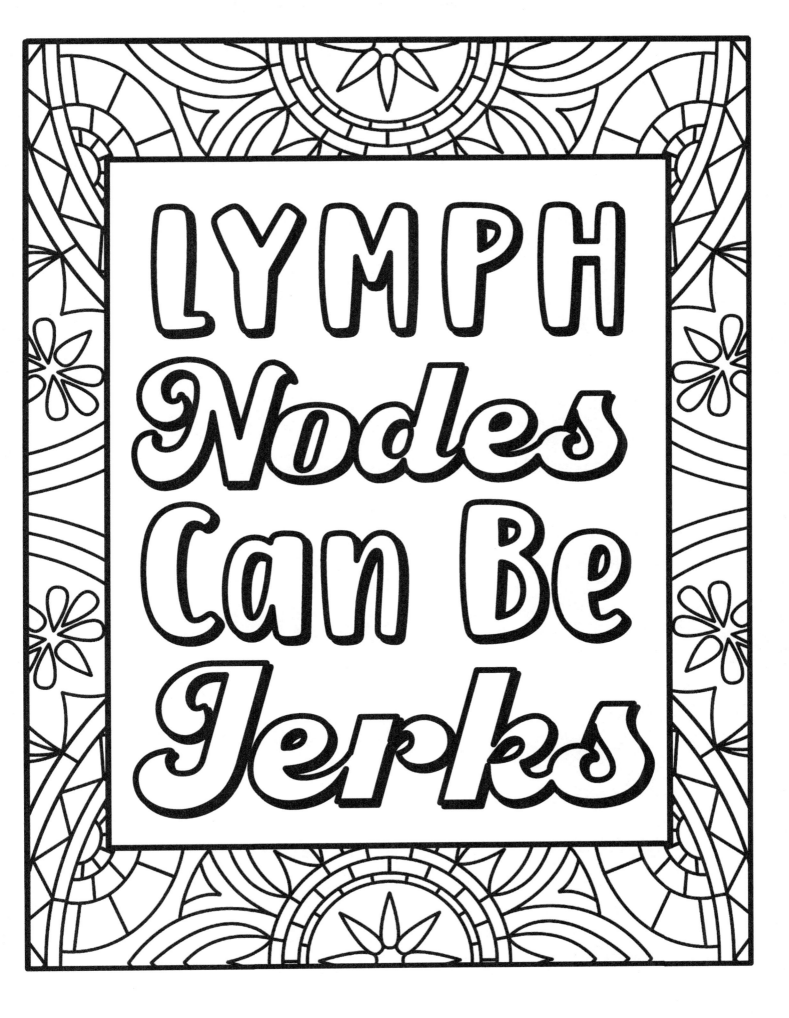

Dear Reader & Colorer,
I hope this coloring book made chemo at least a little bit more tolerable and gave you a few laughs.
F.Y.I. I went through chemo. Twice. Oh, and, did I mention radiation? So, trust me when I say: I plan to be around to kick butt for a very long time! So, go leave that Amazon review, or else!
Pretty please and thank you.
P.S Amazon reviews are what let independent authors and publishers like me to survive!

– K.M. Fredericks